# DUETS FOR VIOLINS

## Second Violin Parts to Selections from Suzuki Violin School Volumes 1, 2, and 3

*Updated to correlate with the International Editions*

## CONTENTS

AMPV: 1.03

© Copyright 2018, 2013, 1971, 1968 International Suzuki Association
Sole publisher for the entire world except Japan: Summy-Birchard, Inc.
Exclusive print rights administered by Alfred Music
All rights reserved. Printed in USA.

ISBN-10: 0-87487-093-3
ISBN-13: 978-0-87487-093-0

2

# 1 Lightly Row

Folk Song

# 2 Song of the Wind

Folk Song

## 3 Go Tell Aunt Rhody

Folk Song

## 4 O Come, Little Children

Folk Song

4

## 5  May Song

Folk Song

## 6  Long, Long Ago

T. H. Bayly

5

5

## 7 Allegro

Shinichi Suzuki

## 8 Perpetual Motion

Shinichi Suzuki

6

# 9 Allegretto

Shinichi Suzuki

# 10 Andantino

Shinichi Suzuki

# 11 Etude

Shinichi Suzuki

# 12 Minuet No. 1

J. S. Bach

# 13 Minuet No. 2

J. S. Bach

# 14 Chorus from "Judas Maccabaeus"

G. F. Handel

# 15 Musette

J. S. Bach

# 16 Bourrée

G. F. Handel

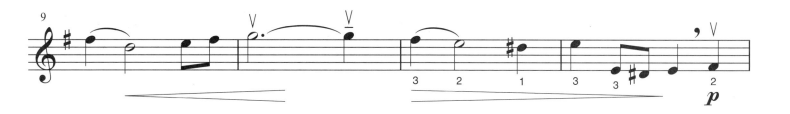

12

# 17 Gavotte

P. Martini

14

# 18 Minuet

**Suzuki Violin School, Vol. 1: Play to \***
**Suzuki Violin School, Vol. 3: Play entire piece**

J. S. Bach

15

**Minuet II**

*D.C. Minuet I al Fine*

# 19 Minuet in G

L. van Beethoven

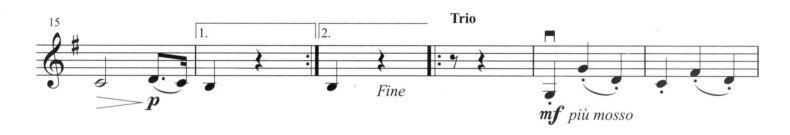

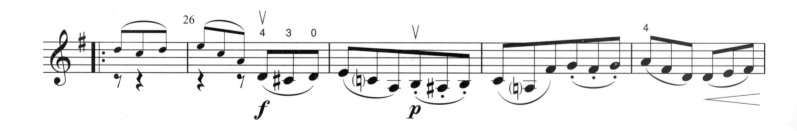

*D.C. al Fine*